CHASITY HOOKS

Travel South Louisiana

Discover the best attractions, food, and activities to explore in Cajun country.

Copyright © 2024 by Chasity Hooks

All rights reserved. No part of this publication may be reproduced, stored or transmitted in any form or by any means, electronic, mechanical, photocopying, recording, scanning, or otherwise without written permission from the publisher. It is illegal to copy this book, post it to a website, or distribute it by any other means without permission.

Chasity Hooks asserts the moral right to be identified as the author of this work.

Chasity Hooks has no responsibility for the persistence or accuracy of URLs for external or third-party Internet Websites referred to in this publication and does not guarantee that any content on such Websites is, or will remain, accurate or appropriate.

Designations used by companies to distinguish their products are often claimed as trademarks. All brand names and product names used in this book and on its cover are trade names, service marks, trademarks and registered trademarks of their respective owners. The publishers and the book are not associated with any product or vendor mentioned in this book. None of the companies referenced within the book have endorsed the book.

First edition

This book was professionally typeset on Reedsy.
Find out more at reedsy.com

The world is a book, and those who do not travel read only a page.

Unknown

Contents

1. Introduction — 1
2. Where exactly is Cajun country? — 3
3. How do you get here? — 5
4. Where should you stay? — 9
5. Where are the best places to eat? — 16
6. What should you do when you get here? — 26
7. What about the nightlife? — 31
8. Where are the festivals & cook-offs? — 34
9. Where should we go shopping? — 38
10. Conclusion — 41
11. Resources — 43

1

Introduction

As a lifelong native of south Louisiana, it has always been one of my greatest joys, to share my home and culture with friends, family and anyone who comes to visit. As Cajuns we love to put on some music, throw open the windows and doors, cook up a big pot of something delicious, and invite friends over to" laissez le bon temp rouler" or let the good times roll. While Lafayette is where I call home, my husband and I love to have what we call "adventure days" where we go out and explore our city and the many surrounding areas; each time experiencing a new restaurant, exhibit, music festival, hike, or tour of something we haven't done before.

I've been blessed to meet many people from all over the country and all walks of life. Many of which, when hearing that I'm from Louisiana, immediately associate the state with one of two things: New Orleans and Mardi Gras, or swamps, alligators, and gumbo. There is so much more to this amazing state and one of the many reasons why when people come to visit, they often don't want to leave.

Louisiana's uniqueness lies in its people, the amazing food, and its resident's exuberant enjoyment of life (Joie des Vivre). Cajuns are strong, proud people who will give you the shirt off their back, lend a hand to a neighbor, love fiercely, and are loyal to a fault. They are generous and kind and never meet a stranger. One of the things my husband quickly learned when he moved to Lafayette, La from Dallas, TX was no matter where you go, someone is going to say hello, ask how you're doing and try to get to know you.

While this guide can in no way include all the thousands of amazing places and things to be discovered in South Louisiana, I have chosen to focus on some of my favorites. I hope these unique places and experiences give you a glimpse into why we love South Louisiana and encourage you to plan a trip to come visit our great state. I promise if you do, you will never be hungry, never stop laughing, and pass one heck of a good time!

2

Where exactly is Cajun country?

Louisiana Parishes

Louisiana, unlike many other states, consists of 64 parishes rather than counties. Cajun Country is made up of 22 parishes across the southeastern part of the boot, commonly referred to as Acadiana. The area comprises prairies, marshlands, swaps, and major cities. No, we don't all live in the swamp with a pet alligator, but some of us do!

This area is as rich in heritage and diverse in culture as the gumbo we serve. The unique communities boast a variety of lifestyles from fishing villages with beautiful natural scenic waterways, to beautiful farmland with horses and rice fields as far as the eye can see, to thriving cities with art galleries, shopping, and some of the best cuisine you have ever experienced.

The word Cajun is adapted from the French-Canadian Acadie. The Cajun people were originally natives of France. In 1604, they began to settle in Acadie, now Nova Scotia as part of France's attempt to colonize Canada. They settled there and excelled at fishing and farming. When the British took over ownership of the colony in the early 1700s, the Acadians refused to play by the British rules (did I mention we were stubborn fiercely independent people). They were exiled by the British with many of them finding their way to south Louisiana, settling in the coastal areas west of New Orleans. Almost 4000 Cajuns had settled in south Louisiana by the early 1800's. They hunted, trapped, and fished the rivers and waterways. Some moved to the prairie lands to raise cattle, rice, cotton, and soybeans. Their French dialect changed to what we lovingly call Cajun French, which was later outlawed from 1921 – 1974 when only English was allowed to be spoken in Louisiana schools. The return of the native French tongue has been slow to resurface as many today work hard to encourage Cajun French speaking in an effort to bring back the culture and the language.

3

How do you get here?

Planes. If you are planning to fly to Cajun country, there are several nearby airports to get you here.

- Louis Armstrong New Orleans International Airport.
- Baton Rouge Metropolitan Airport.
- Lafayette Regional Airport.
- Lake Charles Regional Airport.

Lafayette Regional Airport
  200 Terminal Drive
  Suite 200
  Lafayette, LA 70508-2159
  337-703-4800
  https://lftairport.com/ Terminal Building Hours of Operation: 3:00 a.m. – until the last flight of the day.

The Lafayette Regional Airport (LFT) is right in the heart of Cajun country and has recently undergone a renovation and now includes multiple terminals. For many years it was just one small terminal, but with the recent expansion in 2023, there is now a beautiful new terminal complete with a bar, cold and hot food options, a business center, comfortable seating and plenty of Free Wi-Fi. Porter services, convenient parking, and car rental services are also available. They service flights through American, United, and Delta airlines.

Louis Armstrong New Orleans International Airport
   1 Terminal Drive
   Kenner, LA 70062
   https://flymsy.com/ The airport is open 24 hours daily, including holidays.

Louis Armstrong New Orleans International Airport (MSY) is a rather large airport and grants you access to all things New Orleans which is legendary for its history, food, and good times. MSY provides a passenger-friendly environment that welcomes millions of travelers each year from around the world. The airport boasts numerous restaurants and shopping experiences to make your wait between flights truly enjoyable. They service many airlines including Air Canada, Alaska Airlines, Allegiant Air, American, Avelo, Breeze Airways, British Airways, Delta, Frontier, Jet Blue, Southwest Airlines, Spirit Airlines, Sun Country Airlines, United and Vacation Express.

Lake Charles Regional Airport
   500 Airport Boulevard Suite 104
   Lake Charles, LA 70607
   https://flylakecharles.com/ Terminal Hours – 3:00 am until last flight arrival

The Lake Charles Regional Airport (LCH) provides air service by

HOW DO YOU GET HERE?

United Airlines and American Airlines. United provides service to their Houston hub with connecting flights to virtually anywhere on the globe. American provides service to their Dallas/Fort Worth hub with connecting flights worldwide. LCH is also home to multiple helicopter operators that service medical and offshore oil & gas industries in Louisiana and the Gulf of Mexico.

Baton Rouge Metropolitan Airport
  9430 Jackie Cochran Dr
  Baton Rouge, LA 70807
  https://www.flybtr.com/ Terminal is open 24 hours a day.

The Baton Rouge Metropolitan Airport (BTR) has a state-of-the-art terminal facility with a wide range of passenger amenities. The centerpiece of the terminal is a beautifully landscaped, three-story atrium with a view of the airfield. It also features a food court and gift shops. They service flights through United, American, and Delta.

Trains. If you are looking for a more nostalgic retro experience, you could fly into New Orleans and take an Amtrak passenger train to Lafayette. Amtrak offers routes to New Orleans from many cities across the country.

Automobiles. If you are up for a road trip down south. Interstate 10 spans South Louisiana from East to West. If you are driving through Texas, you will drive straight through Lake Charles. Make sure you stop off and enjoy the view over the lake. If you are coming from the North, Interstate 49 will bring you South. If you have time, stop off in Natchitoches and take a drive along the river. You can view the famous house from the movie **Steel Magnolias** which was filmed in Natchitoches. You can also easily rent vehicles at any of the airports listed above, which is highly recommended to truly explore all of the amazing places in South Louisiana.

4

Where should you stay?

The city of Lafayette in Lafayette parish is a central point for Cajun country and one of the largest cities. Lafayette offers a wide variety of lodging, food and activities with a small-town feel. If you are looking at a map of Louisiana, Lafayette is right in the middle of the state in the southern half.

So where should you stay? I'll share a few of my favorites and some unique offerings. Of course we have our share of chain hotels: Marriott, Hilton, DoubleTree, Candlewood Suites, Staybridge Suites, but if you truly want an experience, immerse yourself in the culture and consider a boutique local hotel or one of the many beautiful bed and breakfast options, or opt for a whole home in a beautiful neighborhood listed on Airbnb, VRBO, Evolve, or Travelocity.

The **Juliet Hotel** at 800 Jefferson Street is a beautiful boutique hotel located in the heart of downtown Lafayette. The hotel offers a complimentary breakfast and is within walking distance to many local restaurants, shopping, and nightlife. https://www.juliethotels.com/ It's the perfect place to land to take in a local concert, have a nice dinner and pick up dessert or coffee at **Carpe Diem Wine & Coffee Bar** just a few doors down from the hotel. https://www.carpediemcafeandwinebar.com/

If you would like a more upscale experience, check out **The Carriage House Hotel** located at 603 Silverstone Rd in Lafayette is nestled in the exclusive high-end development of River Ranch. From the Carriage House, you can walk to nearby local shops and restaurants, or drive to larger retailers just a few blocks away. If you are looking for luxury and convenience, the Carriage House is what you are looking for. https://www.thecarriagehousehotel.com/

On the southern side of Lafayette parish, you will discover **The Cajun Mansion Bed & Breakfast** at 4304 Deacon Rd in Youngsville, Louisiana. Whether you're traveling on business, vacationing or just need a romantic getaway or a girl's getaway, do it in classic style while surrounding yourself in a luxurious environment. This peaceful retreat offers a charming patio for lounging with a refreshing drink in hand. Or indulge in a luxurious massage in the comfort and privacy of your room, every moment is designed to soothe and rejuvenate. Let the serene ambiance and personalized pampering envelop you, making you wish you could stay forever. A complimentary homemade breakfast is served daily.

As they advertise on their website, The Cajun Mansion is in the middle of Cajun Country and minutes from everywhere you would want to visit. You're in the heart of local festivals, swamp & alligator boat tours, Cajun food, dancing & music. The owners welcome French-speaking guests; On parle francais! https://louisianacajunmansion.com/

Mouton Plantation at 338 North Sterling Road in Lafayette is an

WHERE SHOULD YOU STAY?

eight-room bed & breakfast in downtown Lafayette. The Maison Mouton offers a quiet respite from the hustle and bustle of the city while still being centrally located. Originally built in 1820, the Bed & Breakfast resides in a restored Creole house nestled on a quiet street in the Sterling Grove Historic District. The buildings that surround the main plantation are a collection of quaint cottages nestled along an alley of ancient oak trees and surrounded by lush gardens, allowing guests to get lost in the tranquility of the South. Comfortable and romantic, each room is decorated with old- world furnishings offering a glimpse into the lifestyle of the Acadians of the early 1800s. While enjoying the bygone era, the need for modern amenities is not overlooked. https://moutonplantation.com/

For those traveling on a budget the **Blue Moon Saloon & Guest House** located at 215 E. Convent Street in Lafayette, Louisiana offers a variety of single beds, single rooms, or the entire house which all include the use of their fully equipped kitchen. Be entertained with free admission to live local music on the back porch. The fantastic backyard bar and hang out space is complete with swings and hammock spaces. Blue Moon is seated directly across the street from the circa 1940 **Borden's Ice Cream** shop, one of the only remaining Borden's shops in the country. www.bluemoonpresents.com

If you find yourself exploring closer to the western coast of Cajun country consider reserving a room at The Marco Hotel at 401 North Lakeshore Drive in Lake Charles, Louisiana. The Marco is your gateway to Lake Charles' breathtaking beauty. Their newly renovated hotel boasts unrivaled lakefront views, impeccable service, and modern amenities. They are conveniently located and within walking distance to many local restaurants and shopping. Make sure to grab dinner at Steamboat Bills on the lake. https://www.steamboatbillsonthelake.co

m/ or Southern Spice Restaurant and Grill https://eatatsouthernspice.com/. Their homestyle cooking and family friendly atmosphere will make you feel right at home. https://www.themarcohotel.com/.

For a rare treat, time your visit around the **Louisiana Pirate Festival**. This event is a unique opportunity to experience a unique pirate and seafaring festival with events on both land and sea. On the shores of historic Lake Charles, the Louisiana Pirate Festival showcases entertainment by a variety of talented musicians, performers and artists. This family friendly event is complete with cannon demonstrations, costume contests, local arts and crafts, themed souvenirs, games and attractions. https://www.louisianapiratefestival.com/

Also, in the western coastal area you can find a truly unique experience at the **Grosse Savanne Lodge**, located at 1730 Big Pasture Road in Lake Charles. The Grosse Savanne Lodge is found in the Southwest corner of Louisiana in the heart of Cameron Parish. Easily accessible from Interstate 10, the Lodge is midway between Houston & New Orleans approximately 20 minutes south of Lake Charles. This gorgeous mansion has plenty of room to accommodate large groups with its well-appointed 12,000 square feet of space. Seated in the marsh, the mansion is elevated above the landscape providing astounding views of the natural beauty and amenities. What makes it truly special is the 50,000 acres of land that surrounds it. You will find fresh and brackish marshes, coastal prairies, and agricultural lands are all located here. It's a rare find to have access to experience a combination of world class water-fowling, fresh and saltwater fishing, alligator hunting, and eco tours all in the same day. This is a 5-star experience that gives you a glimpse into the unique southwestern Louisiana lifestyle. https://www.grossesavanne.com/

WHERE SHOULD YOU STAY?

North of Lafayette in Evangeline parish is the privately operated boutique hotel in the small town of Mamou. **The Hotel Cazan** (Ca - Zan) located at 401 6th Street in Mamou, Louisiana is in the heart of Mamou's Historic District, at the one and only red light. A few doors down from the hotel is a bakery with delicious cheesecake, as well as several neighborhood Cajun bars. The Hotel Cazan is described as cute, quirky, clean, and eclectic. Every room has a theme, from octopuses and dogs to New Orleans, ships, and even a Supernatural Room with a spooky skeleton that lights up. Each of their seventeen rooms has a showerhead with rainbow colored water. They also boast an elegant bar and 1950s malt shop. https://hotelcazan.com/

On the same block as the hotel is the **World Famous Fred's Lounge.** Saturday mornings at Fred's involve live local music and Cajun dancing, a must see for any visitor to this area. Fred's is a local favorite and a must-stop if you are in the area for Mardi Gras. The Mardi Gras celebration in Mamou is not the commonly known Mardi Gras with beads and debauchery, but rather a true Cajun Mardi gras where participants dress in hand-made costumes and ride horses going house to collect ingredients for a Gumbo which is cooked and shared at a Fais Do Do (Cajun dance party).

While you're in the area, make sure to check out the cute public plaza which hosts a beautiful mural and a fountain, perfect for taking photographs. This is a local favorite for Instagrammers. You will feel as if you have traveled back to a simpler time and place.

To the east of Lafayette, in St. Martin parish you will find a handful of amazing bed and breakfast options. **Maison Madeleine** located at 1015 John D Hebert Road in Breaux Bridge, Louisiana dates back to the 1840s and is on the National Register of Historic Places. Settled among lush gardens on the shores of Lake Martin, this hidden gem is home to one of the largest wading bird rookeries in North America. The cottage has been lovingly restored by owner Madeleine Cenac, and features bousillage walls (a mud and Spanish moss mix) that is authentic to the original method of home building by our Cajun ancestors. Charming and rustic, this place is utterly Cajun. They offer a variety of accommodations and complimentary hot breakfasts. They even offer cooking classes and private catered dinners. https://www.maisonmadeleine.com/

The nearby small town of Breaux Bridge is one of the cultural centers of Acadiana and the heartland of the inviting Cajun way of life. Breaux Bridge offers a wide variety of flea markets and antique stores as well as local restaurants with live music. This small town is home to the Crawfish festival which happens each May.

The Cajun Getaway is an affordable quaint villa complex located at 427 Broussard Street in Breaux Bridge, Louisiana which is 11 miles from the city of Lafayette. They provide air-conditioned units with coffee makers, microwave, toaster, flat-screen TVs, a terrace, and private bathroom. They also offer a selection of food options including warm dishes, local specialties, and fresh pastries for breakfast. https://www.booking.com/hotel/us/cajun-french-get-away.html

In Abbeville, located in Vermilion parish you will find **The Caldwell House** at 105 East Vermilion Street. Seated in Historic Downtown Abbeville, The Caldwell is an excellent way to experience Cajun History, food, and music festivals. This bed and breakfast is the perfect setting for a true Cajun country getaway. They can accommodate vacation rentals and special events and offer a superb southern breakfast with selections such as their famous Pecan Praline French toast. If your day

WHERE SHOULD YOU STAY?

starts early, they even offer continental breakfast boxes to go. https://thecaldwell.com/

In Iberia parish, you can find a true gem. **The Olive Branch Cottages** at 6008 Old Jeanerette Rd (Hwy 87) in New Iberia offer a stay in an original cypress shotgun house that dates back almost 100 years. Here you can experience the rich heritage and traditions that began in the eighteenth century. The Cottages previously served as housing quarters for farm workers on the Duhe family sugar cane farm. During your stay fill your itinerary with unique Louisiana events, bayou tours, and trips to exotic islands. Enjoy lush tropical garden tours, famous factory tours, museums, an award-winning main street, stately plantation homes, art galleries, live theater, shopping, fishing, walking tours, swamp tours, boating, golfing, birding, canoeing, festivals, exquisite cuisine, scenic drives and more .https://olivebranchcottages.com

5

Where are the best places to eat?

Should you find yourself in a conversation with a Cajun and you ask them their favorite place to eat, more than likely you are going to hear, "At my house". I have to say, I'm in this same boat. Most of us are amazing cooks and love to see the joy on someone's face when they taste something so unexpectedly good. If you can wrangle an invite to someone's house for supper, you should definitely take them up on it. Until that happens, south Louisiana has no shortage of amazing places to eat. Whether you are dining on a budget or ready to celebrate with something more lavish the choices are endless. Restaurants offer fresh locally caught seafood, locally sourced meats, and many farm to table produce options. Here are a few of our favorites from the area.

Dwyers Café at 323 Jefferson Street in Lafayette is a local favorite. It's a great place to grab breakfast, sit and enjoy a cup of coffee, and soak in the surrounding conversations. For lunch they offer a variety of plate lunch options ranging from roast meats, smothered chicken, pork chops, stuffed bell pepper, seafood and vegetables.

The French Press at 214 E. Vermilion Street in Lafayette is a favorite

WHERE ARE THE BEST PLACES TO EAT?

place for weekend brunch or a quick lunch. They serve innovative versions of traditional Cajun and American cuisine with a focus on fresh, high-quality ingredients and rich flavors. Local favorites include the Cajun Benedict and the Sweet Baby breezes which is a buttermilk biscuit with a fried boudin ball, a slice of bacon, and Steen's cane syrup. Trust me, just try it!

My favorite way to kick off a weekend is Friday lunch at **Olde Tyme Grocery** at 218 W. Saint Mary Boulevard in Lafayette. You cannot go wrong choosing a messy meatball, roast beef. or Shrimp Po-boy from Olde Tyme. It's tradition in our house when friends come to visit for Festival International, the first stop is Olde Tyme for a Shrimp Po Boy to kick off the festival weekend. This is one of the oldest and in my opinion, best po-boy shops in town.

If you are hungry for smoked meats, try **Johnson's Boucaniere** at 1111 Saint John Street in Lafayette. Johnson's is a family-owned smokehouse. They offer smoked sausage and boudin, smoked pork roasts, brisket, and country style ribs and serve plate lunches daily. The brisket grilled cheese is a must try.

Tchoup's MidCIty Restaurant & Bar at 117 S. College Road in Lafayette is located in an old house that has been converted into a local BBQ restaurant & bar. The atmosphere feels like you're eating at your grandma's house. The bar is super cute and cozy, and the backyard has a huge deck under the oak tree with yard space for the kids and dogs. This is a great place to grab brunch on the weekend or lunch & dinner.

For more traditional Cajun fare, **Bon Temp Grill** at 1211 Pinhook Road in Lafayette offers swamp edge cuisine in an urban Cajun atmosphere.

Their chef inspired dishes feed the need for true Cajun delicacies without the upscale prices. They also have live music seven days a week and offer a well thought out cocktail menu.

For a nice dinner or a special celebration, **Charley G's Seafood & Grill** at 3809 Ambassador Caffery Pkwy in Lafayette fits the bill. Their award-winning chef excels at creating unique and vibrant dishes with local aged beef and local seafood. The service is impeccable and the nightly piano music in the bar is a nice backdrop to any date.

At 240 Tubing Road in Broussard, you will find **Poor Boy's Riverside Inn**. This family-owned business has successfully served our community for over eighty-nine years. As you approach the restaurant you will see a miniature version of a Louisiana swamp and oil rig. Their menu is excellent and the Lump crab meat in butter and Crabbie's appetizer are a must try.

In Saint Landry parish, **Café Josephine** at 818 Napoleon Avenue in Sunset is a laid back, rustic atmosphere serving southern cuisine prepared with farm fresh ingredients and gulf seafood. Locals rave about the oysters.

WHERE ARE THE BEST PLACES TO EAT?

Traditional King Cake

One of our favorite things about Mardi Gras is King Cake. King cake is first served on King's Day (January 6) and lasts through the eve of Mardi Gras to celebrate the three kings who came to visit Jesus. The cake is a sugared yeast bread ring covered in a glaze. Hidden in the cake's interior or under a slice, is a small plastic baby which symbolizes luck and prosperity. The tradition says that whoever finds the baby has to buy the next King cake. Every town and every baker creates their own delicious version of this confection. In my opinion, **Keller's Bakery Downtown** at 1012 Jefferson Street in Lafayette is one of the best. Established in 1929, Keller's offers a wide variety of cakes, pies, and delectable treats. The Walnut Amaretto is my personal favorite.

Gumbo is another local favorite that can be made in a million different ways. Every person has their favorite recipe. Gumbo is a thick, hearty, roux-based stew that is eaten as a soup over rice. Chicken and sausage, seafood, shrimp and okra, duck and andouille are just a short list of gumbo versions you will find during your visit here. Restaurant gumbo is just as diverse as those made at someone's home. **Rachael's Café** at 104 Republic Avenue in Lafayette is a family-owned café that serves up some of the best seafood dishes as well as health Cajun, creole, vegetarian and gluten-free options. You will want to try the seafood or chicken and sausage gumbo! YUM

Chicken & Sausage Gumbo

I haven't met a Cajun yet, who doesn't appreciate a good Seafood Buffet. **Lagneaux's Restaurant & Meat Market** at 445 Ridge Road in Lafayette.is a family-owned business established in 1965 and is known for a delicious seafood buffet, seafood platters, crawfish dinners, gumbos, boiled crawfish, and crabs. Their market is also known for great boudin, cracklins, smoked and fresh sausage, beef jerky, steaks, and specialty meats.

No seafood dinner is complete without a delicious tray of salty raw or charbroiled oysters. **Uncle T's Oyster Bar** at 1001 Saint Mary Street is located along the train tracks in the art district of Scott. This locally owned establishment serves authentic Louisiana seafood, po-boys, raw, and charbroiled oysters.

An absolute must do when you visit Cajun country is the Zydeco breakfast at **Buck and Johnny's** located at 100 Berard Street in Breaux Bridge. A unique restaurant blending the boldness of Cajun spice with the rich smooth flavors of Italy. Offering live local music every week, Buck and Johnny's hosts the famous Zydeco breakfast every Saturday morning. It's a wonderful way to fill your belly with a seafood omelet and dance a little cajun two-step.

Also in Breaux Bridge is **Café Sydnie Mae** located at 140 E Bridge Street. Take in some of the unique antique shops Breaux Bridge has to offer and grab some lunch or brunch with a side of local music, great food & drinks. The red beans and rice with fried catfish are just like grandma used to make!

One of our favorite ways to spend time and hang out with friends is at a crawfish or shrimp boil. When done at someone's home, this is a backyard party like no other. Seasoned boiled seafood and vegetables are spread on a table and eaten family style with cold beverages and good conversation. To avoid the messy clean-up, there are many restaurants that serve up these delicacies when they are in season. **Cajun Claws Seafood Boilers** at 175 Frontage Road in Rayne is a Family style restaurant with a relaxed atmosphere. They offer a full menu and some of the best boiled seafood around. Whether you choose crawfish, shrimp, snow crab, blue crab, or dungeness crab, your palette will be overjoyed.

A fun way to spend an afternoon is a visit to **Vermilionville**. The historic folk life park offers a look into the past of the history, culture, and natural resources of the Native Americans, Acadians, Creoles, and peoples of African descent. They offer educational tours, a Cajun dancehall with live music, and a wonderful restaurant on the property.

La Cuisine de Maman at Vermilionville is a full-service restaurant serving Cajun and creole cuisine set in a 19th century folklife and heritage park. Their biscuits are a must have!

Don's Seafood at 4309 Johnston Street in Lafayette is a long-standing 80-year icon started by the Landry Family. It is a local favorite and often packed on most nights for dinner. To cool off on a hot afternoon, visit the bar at Don's for some of the coldest beer on tap. Pair that with a plate of oysters or their crispy buttery hush puppies. C'est si bon! (It's so good)

South Louisiana has so many truly unique and delicious restaurants, but locals know that some of the best food on the go can be found in our gas stations and local country stores. Seriously! Some of the best BBQ you will ever eat can be found at a gas station. If you walk into a station and smell BBQ grab yourself a rib or two.

Although it is a little out of the way at 13923 La 35 in Kaplan, **Suire's Grocery & Restaurant** is a must-stop. Known by hunters and fishermen as a great place to restock and grab a bite on the way to a fishing or hunting camp, Suire's serves up home-cooked Louisiana Cajun food and lots of it. For nearly 50 years this iconic store has served up Cajun cuisine like turtle stew, catfish, boudin, sandwiches, BBQ burgers, and fried seafood. Their daily plate lunches are great for the budget with ample portions and equal amounts of hospitality and love.

All great southern salesmen know that a great way to reward or thank your clients is to show up at their office on a Friday morning with donuts, kolaches, or a platter of cracklins and boudin. Cracklins are a Cajun delicacy of pork skin and meat fried crisp. **Katchner's Specialty**

Meats at 312 LA 93 in Scott offers a variety of ready-to-eat foods, boudin, sausage, specialty meats, pork and chicken cracklin, and frozen meals to cook at home.

Cracklins and boudin, like a lot of Cajun, food vary from location to location. **The Best Stop** at 625 Hwy 93 N in Scott has been serving Acadiana for over thirty-eight years. This Specialty Meat store serves fresh and smoked sausage, boudin, cracklins, specialty meats, and more.

After a few days in Cajun country, you may be interested in some other non-Cajun options. **Scratch Farm Kitchen** at 2918 Johnston Street in Lafayette creates magic with locally sourced meats and vegetables. They offer a unique menu of farm-to-table delicacies including vegetarian and gluten-free options.

Pizza with a Cajun flare is how **Dean-O's Pizza** at 305 Bertrand Drive in Lafayette has established themselves as a local favorite with adults and kids alike. The shrimp a'la Deanos, Marie Laveau, and T-Rex are just a few pizza favorites. Can't make up your mind, that's okay, they let you mix up to four options on one pie.

Farm fresh seasonally evolving menus within a curated retail space is what you will find at **5-Mile Eatery.** Located at 317 Heymann Blvd in Lafayette this hot new establishment offers Organic Wholesome Fare for breakfast and lunch.

Hideaway on Lee is an old house converted into a bar/restaurant/music venue. Located at 407 Lee Avenue in Lafayette, their menu consists of classic americana, with both classic and regionally creative burgers and a seasonally driven classic and original cocktail menu.

WHERE ARE THE BEST PLACES TO EAT?

At 431 Jefferson Street in Lafayette, you will find a modern approach to the nostalgic soda shop. **Sunday's Soda Fountain** offers unique ice cream concoctions both tame and spiked as well as a full menu. We love to stop in for an afternoon snack or to grab dinner and dessert after a show.

Tsunami Sushi at 412 Jefferson Street in Lafayette was one of the first sushi restaurants in town. With fresh seafood and diverse Asian dishes, their menu marries the owner's Japanese and Eastern flare with southern roots. They offer standard sushi rolls, nigiri, and sashimi. Many of the sushi selections come with a little South Louisiana enhancement. They also serve grilled fish, chicken, and pork.

From their humble food truck beginnings, **Viva La Waffle** has grown to a fully established restaurant at 101 Liberty Ave in Lafayette. You will find a unique offering of waffle sandwiches with various toppings. Great for breakfast, lunch, or dinner. My personal favorite is the figgy piggy, a delicious combination of candied figs and prosciutto on a buttermilk waffle.

Athena's Express located at 2133 Kaliste Saloom Rd in Lafayette is found inside the USA Food Express gas station. Again, some of the best meals can be found at the gas station. They serve a variety of Greek & Lebanese food made fresh daily. For a good variety try the Athena special plate for two which is loaded with gyro, chicken shawarma, feta salad, kibbe and grape leaves.

6

What should you do when you get here?

As the locals say, if you can't find something to do here, then you aren't looking! There truly is something for everyone in South Louisiana. These great outdoor options are a great way to see natural Louisiana wildlife and experience a little history of our area.

You can explore the Atchafalaya (A-Cha-Fa-Lie-A) swamp by tour boat or airboat at **MaGee's Louisiana Swamp & Airboat Tours** located at 1337 Henderson Levee Road in Henderson. If you are interested in Kayaking, this is also a great place to launch a Kayak. The guides are knowledgeable and well versed in the area. They do a fantastic job of explaining the ecosystem and ways of the swamp as well as providing some entertaining stories.

WHAT SHOULD YOU DO WHEN YOU GET HERE?

The Nature Conservancy's Cypress Island Preserve at 1264 Prairie Highway in Saint Martinville serves as a centerpiece for viewing Louisiana wildlife. You can see everything that represents a cypress swamp in Louisiana. The 9000-acre preserve is home to alligators, birds, and other wildlife. They offer a 2.5-mile walking trail suitable for ages 5 and up. Great place for bird watching, hiking, boating and kayaking.

Louisiana's Creole Nature Trail is an opportunity to experience the untamed natural wonders near Lake Charles at 2740 Ruth Street in Sulphur. You can tour Coastal wetlands, wildlife refuges, and marshes. Appreciate the surrounding wildlife such as alligators, birding, and crabbing/shrimping. Make sure to bring your camera, hat, sunscreen, and a fishing pole.

For a day of family fun, visit **The Zoo of Acadiana (Zoosiana)** at 5601 Hwy 90 E in Broussard. See wildlife from all around the world in a fun learning experience complete with a petting zoo and safari train.

For a nice hike through gorgeous gardens, you will want to tour **Rip Van Winkle Gardens** at 5505 Rip Van Winkle Road in New Iberia. Book a tour to view their beautiful secret garden which is drivable but there are a few spots you will want to stop and walk around. Enjoy lunch at the Café Jefferson overlooking the gardens and Lake Peigneur.

Eunice Depot Museum is located in an old train depot that was originally established in 1894. It contains exhibits and collections depicting the lifestyles of the early settlers of the prairie town of Eunice. They also offer a free Cajun French class once a month. You can see the exhibits at 220 South C C Duson Street in Eunice.

Houma's House Estate & Gardens at 40136 Highway 942 in Darrow offers a chance to experience a historic plantation house and tour the Great River Road Museum or enjoy a self-guided tour through their 38-acre gardens.

Acadiana Park Nature Station is a great place to explore hiking trails along the Vermilion River. Located at 1205 E. Alexander Street in Lafayette.

If you are looking for more family-friendly experiences the **Children's Museum of Acadiana** at 201 E. Congress Street in Lafayette offers over 15 different interactive exhibits for your little ones to enjoy.

Close by the Children's Museum is the **Lafayette Science Museum** at 433 Jefferson Street in Lafayette. The Science Museum hosts a multitude

WHAT SHOULD YOU DO WHEN YOU GET HERE?

of exhibits and a cutting-edge planetarium for visitors of every age.

Moncus Park at 2913 Johnston Street is Lafayette's newest and most interactive park. The park offers a large number of things to do including a playground and splash pad, an adult-size family treehouse that showcases an entire view of the park, live oak trees, hills, walking trails, a fishing pier, an Amphitheater, picnic areas, shaded seating, and hammock area. Moncus Park is also home to the weekly Saturday morning Farmers & Artisans market which is a unique opportunity to pick up local arts & crafts, sample local food vendors, or shop for fresh local meat, seafood, and produce.

Founded in 1975, the **Acadiana Center for the Arts** located at 101 W. Vermilion Street in Lafayette fosters art and culture in Acadiana through the creation of new works of art, exhibits, festivals, performances, and public art.

A great way to wear out the kiddos is to spend some time at the **Kart Ranch Family Fun Center** at 508 Youngsville Hwy in Lafayette. Kart Ranch offers go-karts, water wares, mini golf, and a huge arcade for hours of family fun.

Parc San Souci at 201 East Vermilion in Lafayette is home to a splash pad, skate park, playground, and outdoor live music events. Each Friday evening in the spring and the fall, this park and the adjacent Parc International are bustling with live music, and local food and beverage vendors providing a free night out for visitors.

Planet Ice at 4317 Johnston St in Lafayette is an indoor Ice Hockey & Skating Rink. They offer party rooms, & concessions and are home to the Lafayette Drillers Ice Hockey Team.

The Cypremort Point State Park is one of the few locations near the Gulf of Mexico that can be reached by car. Located at 306 Beach Lane in Cypremort Point, this ½ mile stretch of man-made beach provides a delightful area for relaxing, picnicking, and enjoying the water. There is an opportunity for fishing, crabbing, water skiing, windsurfing, and sailing. The sunsets here are spectacular and no better place to truly witness the glory of God!

7

What about the nightlife?

I f you still have some energy after all these fun-filled days, we've got your evenings covered as well.

Downtown Alive is held in downtown Lafayette in either Parc International at 200 Garfield Street in Lafayette or the adjacent Parc San Souci. This free outdoor concert series takes place on Friday nights during the spring and fall. The entire family can enjoy all types of local music, food, and beverages.

Rhythms on the River is a six-week outdoor free concert series held on Thursday evenings in the spring and fall in River Ranch at 1100 Camellia Blvd in Lafayette. This street party entails entertainment from local musicians, plenty of food and beverages and some great people watching.

Adopted Dog Brewing at 329 Dulles Drive in Lafayette, is one of the newly established local breweries offering music, entertainment, food, and great local craft beers. During the week you can also be entertained by local comedians or even try your hand at some trivia.

Bayou Teche Brewing at 1002 Noth Lane in Arnaudville, LA 70512 offers a Tap Room and beer garden. They serve a large selection of local craft beers and wood-fired pizza.

Lafayette's oldest pool hall is a great place to have a burger, hang out with friends and play pool in a clean smoke free environment. **Max's pool hall** at 105 Kaliste Saloom Road in Lafayette has one of the best chili cheese burgers in town, cold beer and nice billiard tables.

The **Grouse room** is a premier music venue featuring live music, food, cocktails, and great atmosphere. Located at 417 Jefferson Street in Lafayette, this Prohibition-era speakeasy-inspired watering hole combines old school elegance with a modern twist. You can hear talented local musicians playing here several nights each week.

Rock N Bowl is a great place to bowl a few, have a cocktail, grab a snack, and see some awesome live music. Located at 905 Jefferson Street in Lafayette, this bowling alley/music venue is located across the street from the Juliet Hotel.

The Stage Karaoke Bar at 2921 Verot School Road in Lafayette is a great place to sing some tunes in a fun environment. When you are done with your center stage performance, enjoy a cocktail on the patio.

We cannot forget the art scene, **Cite Des Arts** at 109 Vine Street in Lafayette is home to Lafayette's theater community offering a wide variety of plays, comedy shows, live music, and a variety of reading series.

The **Heymann Center** auditorium at 1373 S. College Rd in Lafayette, is home to Broadway musicals, popular concerts, symphony theater,

WHAT ABOUT THE NIGHTLIFE?

and more.

At 505 North Parkerson Avenue in Crowley, you will find **The Grand Opera House of the South**. The Grand Opera house is a uniquely crafted second story opera house built in 1901. This state of the art performing arts venue offers plays and live music events.

For the ultimate food and culture experience, check out the **Cajun Food Tours**. Experience a taste of South Louisiana by bus. This tour stops at 5 locally owned authentic Cajun eateries. Discover the unique history and fall in love with the food and culture of Cajun Country.

For sports fans, spend an afternoon watching the University of Louisiana at Lafayette college athletes compete in football, basketball, baseball, and softball. You can find more details here: https://ragincajuns.com/

Into Horse racing? We've got you covered there as well. **Evangeline Downs Racetrack and Casino** at 2235 Creswell Lane in Opelousas is host to horseracing, dining, live entertainment, and casino gambling in the heart of Cajun country.

8

Where are the festivals & cook-offs?

In South Louisiana there is quite literally a festival for everything: Cajun music, frogs, crawfish, boudin, shrimp, oysters, cracklins, and rice are just a few. Throughout each year there are over 400 festivals inspired by food, music, history, and holidays that occur throughout the state. Most take place over three to five days so you have plenty of time to schedule those in. Festivals occur outside in the spring and the fall as summers in Louisiana tend to be sweltering and no one wants to go outside unless it's to the swimming pool. At all of the festivals, you will find plenty of good food, great music, fun people watching, and the festival outfits are quite entertaining. I'm going to share a handful of my local favorite festivals, but you can find a complete listing here: https://www.explorelouisiana.com/festivals-events-louisiana

I think the first one every one associates with Louisiana is of course, **Mardi Gras**. Now Mardi Gras is not just limited to New Orleans, every southern town has its own version. The Mardi Gras celebrations in Lafayette, Opelousas, Lake Charles, and Houma tend to be a little more family-friendly with parades, carnival rides, and attractions.

Mamou, Eunice, and Church Point offer a chance to experience a more traditional Cajun Mardi Gras with horse rides, chicken chasing, gumbo making, and a traditional Cajun dance or fais do do. Events, balls, and parades are held throughout January and February. The actual date for Mardi Gras changes every year depending on the Lenten season and celebrations can take place over a couple of months.

On the last weekend in April, the barricades go up in downtown Lafayette as the city gets ready to welcome over 300,000 visitors for **Festival International De Louisiane.** This five-day International, free music festival transforms downtown Lafayette into a cultural celebration of music, food, crafts, and entertainment over six blocks of downtown. Over the last twenty years of attending this festival, I have discovered new favorite musicians from Ireland, South Africa, Canada,

Wales, Zimbabwe and France.

The first weekend in May, venture out to Breaux Bridge for the **Crawfish Festival.** If you have ever wanted to try Crawfish this is your opportunity to try it in a variety of ways and all done in one place. While you enjoy those delectable crawfish, you can hear famous Cajun musicians entertaining you with Cajun, Zydeco, and Swamp Pop music. This three-day festival is truly fun for the entire family.

The **Shrimp Festival** takes place in Delcambre, Louisiana every August. The town of Delcambre is located about 20 miles southwest of Lafayette and is home to one of the most productive shrimp fleets. The town devotes an entire weekend honoring its economic lifeblood. Events include a shrimp cook-off, queens pageant, fais-do-do's, food booths, carnival rides, and a blessing of the shrimp boat fleet for the following year. There is plenty of fun and lots to see, hear and eat!

WHERE ARE THE FESTIVALS & COOK-OFFS?

Head down to New Iberia in September for the **Louisiana Sugar Cane Festival** for parades, Cajun and Zydeco music, car show, sugar history, and artistry competitions, horticulture show, and more.

October is a popular festival month and hosts the **Roberts Cove German Fest** in Rayne Louisiana, which celebrates the German heritage of the Roberts Cove area. They offer live entertainment, authentic German food, a large selection of German beer on tap, folklore demonstrations, and Kinderland (kiddie area).

The **Black Pot Festival and Cook Off** at Vermilionville in Lafayette is a celebration of Southern music and food. You may be wondering why we would celebrate a black pot. Well, this is no ordinary black pot, the black cast iron pot is a staple in Cajun cooking. Some of the best jambalaya, etouffee, or sauce piquant can only be made well if it's done in a black pot. If you ever attend an event and there is a large cast iron pot simmering outside, you know you are about to eat something yummy.

Festival Acadiane et Creole at Girard Park in Lafayette is one of the largest free music festivals. This three-day event celebrates Cajun and Creole culture with music, dancing, food, crafts, and a true immersion into the Cajun and Creole experience. What more could you want?

In Saint Landry parish, the small town of Port Barre is host to the **Cracklin Festival**. This festival is held every year on the second weekend in November and is the main fundraiser for the Port Barre Lions club. This three-day festival features cracklin cooking competitions, food, live music, and carnival rides. A cracklin is a fried piece of pork fat with meat and skin still attached. When seasoned and cooked well, they are a crispy Cajun delicacy that melts in your mouth.

9

Where should we go shopping ?

After all of these great tours and festivals, you may want to take home a little piece of Cajun Country. Here are a few unique options for local shopping.

The Lafayette Farmers & Artisans Market takes place every Saturday morning from 8 am until 12 noon. You can shop local, at the Lafayette Farmers & Artisans Market at Moncus Park. The market features local vendors selling meat, seafood, produce, and hot food as well as art, jewelry, and assorted other unique crafts. Often, there are live musicians playing while you shop. About a mile past Moncus Park, where the farmers market takes place. you will find **The Pink Paisley** at 101 Arnould Blvd. Started in 2008, this fun little boutique is one of Lafayette's premier gift stores providing quality gifts at reasonable prices. You can find local gifts, jewelry, home decor, religious gifts, and men's products. Be sure to take home one of their uniquely created t-shirts with Cajun phrases such as Mais La (as if) or Lagniappe -Cause I'm a little Extra.

WHERE SHOULD WE GO SHOPPING?

Along Jefferson Street in downtown Lafayette, you will find a nice variety of shops to explore. **Beausoleil Bookstore** is a quaint little bookstore featuring local, regional, and national selections. Their cute decor and friendly staff make you want to spend the afternoon in a comfy chair reading a great book.

Just a few doors down is **Parish Ink,** another local favorite offering a large selection of clothing and stickers with local art and Cajunisms. Directly across the street, you will find **Rukus Board** shop which is a great place to find skateboarding items for the skaters in your family and the **Lagniappe Record** store. A visit to the **Lagniappe record** store is like stepping back in time when the only way we could get new music was to wait for the album to come out. This locally owned establishment has a large assortment of LP's and 45's that you probably haven't seen in a while.

Take a walk through **Genterie Supply Company**, originally started as a men's clothing store, they now offer clothing for women, home and barware, books, and children's apparel. If you are in the market for vintage clothing, check out **Advintage Thrifts** or **Lilou**. **The Cajun Hatter** offers authentic handmade hats with natural materials and traditional crafting.

At 501 Jefferson you will find **Hub City Cycles,** a mom-and-pop bike shop specializing in new and used bike sales and bike repair. One of my personal favorite places to shop is **Adorn.** This local boutique specializes in handcrafted jewelry, apparel, and accessories.

On the South side of Lafayette, is a one stop Louisiana shop. **Louisiana Hot Stuff** at 4409 Ambassador Caffery Pkwy is a great place to pick up souvenirs, local favorites, and sports apparel.

Big Boys Toys & Hobbies at 2930 Johnston Street offers quality toys and hobbies for kids from one to one hundred. This locally owned toy and hobby store offers tons of fun for all ages. With shelves fully stocked with nostalgic board games, toys, modern remote-control cars, and accessories, you can definitely find something to keep the family entertained.

10

Conclusion

Adventure Day

Whether you come here to immerse yourself in our rich heritage and culture, experiment with exotic delicious Cajun food, or learn to dance the Cajun two-step, your trip to South Louisiana will change you. I hope when you leave you take away a little piece of the slower-paced joy of life we enjoy, a new recipe to wow your friends, or just some great stories of your experiences in the state we love. If you found this guide helpful, your positive review would be greatly appreciated. Au revoir mon ami, à la prochaine! (Goodbye my friends, until next time)

11

Resources

Louisiana Destinations | Tour Louisiana. (n.d.). https://www.tourlouisiana.com/regions/cajun-country

Gage, E. N. (2021, July 19). Louisiana's Cajun Country Is So Much More Than Gumbo and Gators — Though They've Got Those, Too. *Travel + Leisure*. https://www.travelandleisure.com/trip-ideas/acadiana-louisiana-cajun-country-road-trip

Visit Lake Charles | OFFICIAL travel guide of Southwest Louisiana. (n.d.). https://www.visitlakecharles.org/

Breaux Bridge. (n.d.). Louisiana Official Travel and Tourism Information. https://www.explorelouisiana.com/cities/breaux-bridge

Things to do | Evangeline Parish Tourism | Louisiana. (n.d.). EP Tourism. https://www.evangelineparishtourism.org/

Lafayette hotels & things to do | Lafayette Vacations. (n.d.). https://www.lafayettetravel.com/

acadiatourism.org. (2024, January 17). Home - acadiatourism.org. https://acadiatourism.org/

Evolve | Authentic vacation rental homes you can count on. (n.d.). https://www.evolve.com/

Airbnb | Holiday rentals, cabins, beach houses & more. (n.d.). Airbnb. https://www.airbnb.com/

LaDOTD - Aviation. (n.d.). https://wwwapps.dotd.la.gov/multimodal/aviation/airportdirectory.aspx

Made in the USA
Coppell, TX
29 April 2025

48826132R00030